Death & Disaster Series

M ONK

BOOKS

Death &
Disaster
Series

Lonely Christopher

Monk Books — New York — MMXIV

Monk Books
626 Park Place
Brooklyn, NY 11238
monk-books.com

Cover Photo, "Exhaust Trail of STS-51-L," Courtesy of NASA
Interior design by Ben Pease
Cover design by Lonely Christopher and Ben Pease

First Edition, 2014
ISBN-13: 978-0-9913221-0-7
Printed in the United States of America

The Order

"Everything must have an ending except my love for you."
—Samuel M. Johnson, *Einstein on the Beach*

Poems in June

Easy Poem in June

Not like you
I like climbing down a ladder
made of gold into
Hell
some people have died
for this country.

You Have Ideals

You have ideals and I
have June
June is not an aspiration
but a thing to suffer
so I have June
you take whatever you like.
There is no Christian God.

Blow Up

See the girl in her hijab
she blew up.
America in June.

I

I am doing
going about your work
as the world goes
into its gross June
against us
in economy.

Desperation

I have no tract and nothing
beyond this June this rubric
set up and forsaken, unborn
all I want to be a human again
for the first time known famous
people touched the poet's feet
made me famous made mom's
hair fall out fall out again and
again how does this happen in
June how does one write in June
in this sick planet I want to be
famous I want the poet's fame
rub off of my feet talk to people
drink spend money
June
six people shot dead through the
skull on one side of the street I fly
down with unknown dreams opposite
now mother has cancer dad is
depressed brother gives birth
in June in the sound of the others
there are only three people
three people you can trust
and even then
look what
happens
to them.

June Emotional Poem

Try and concentrate
on that plot of land
where things happened
till they razed it and
built a new America I
don't belong in America
I belong in love and scorn
and processes
to process it
and make it less than complete
your lovers
all are your mother
your mother
has chemicals
your chemicals
gave up.
Give up. Sell
your books. You
won't be recognized
your qualities
will all super markets.

Hunger

Coughing up blood
is there not one precious
that gives permission.

Black June

No California.
The sky blackens
turns slack
the tongue of your joy
lasts
and then it's not
going down anymore
the smudges apparent
on the side of my burning
inside of your long and
the sweat on a lemonade glass.

A & Q

We must tell
lies how else
does the sky
sward green
how do they
die like they
do.

Button

Ryan I think of you
Susan dear heal you
the poverty of gaze
the hospital blanket
warm pressed it's warm
Ryan what are you doing
Ryan where are you what
do you think of me when
Susan thank you
I will take you with me
neglected into best love
Susan pray for yourself
pray you undo this button
it's not in here.

Saturday in June

Thrown the pudding into the bushes
June vituperates
drizzle under the sun
accepted in possible
the brick door
the sidewalk is white
sleep paralysis
think of the people along
mind if I in my garret
bard and cry up weather
the wind around necks
the tawdry hats the ladies
never mind.

Âge D'or

Pastoral demagogue
for the scalding information
collapses all into the June.
It's weird getting older.

Westfield

I will be polite in the house
where I was born and kept
writing—soldiers of the cross
lately capitalism
be the greatest grace
in your obscenity
doctors who let this
make me puke
make me take a gun
and turn it against scenery
tracing over the side of
finding it
finding it and sort of ignoring
it letting it eat you
eat your soul out.
I was born in Westfield
and I don't know my mom.

The Lollipop Aftermath of the Night Before

With you in all considerations
am I not but to believe
the floral print of your appointment
shall I so depraved succor on the rich
shall you do something sexy for me
fuck me up the ass
for a moment or two
whilst mother dies
and she is
and society governs
by God it surely does
it has its rules
but no power
where does that power come from
that moves us all, dying?
I love a boy's cock   ·
it makes me think of AIDS
it gets me off.
My mother dies.
Susan I can't think about you
till I see you well enough
inside it
and around
my God
death just think of it my G-d.

Untitled Poem

I, too slack and stupid
to write any more.

June's Harp

June's harp
makes an unrecoverable sound
all the teeth fall out;
failed return to a neighbor's bed
thick with little cockroaches.

Make Art

What does art tell us about
how they told her there was
nothing left to do told her to
go home and die. What does
art tell us about how she has
decided to seek alternative
treatment by going to some
guy's house to sit in a magic
box in Sloatsburg, New York.
What does art tell us about
I don't know   I don't know
make art.

June

We put Gandhi on money
we put a soft hell
in the Orphic spleen
all goes that way
will you drink this.

June Narcissus

I will write poetry while you die
then I will die
then poetry will write itself.

June Promises

Money makes my hand move
the promise
in June
go fuck yourself sideways
and never win
think you live a good life
and suck on gasoline.

Eternity

There is a new shape
to tremble before to
terrible anew
there is a sound in the
sky there is an amaranth
that will
tiny particles the clouds
baby prizes the things you
took
you took from me.
Do not face eternity with your brain.

Happiness in June

You can be if you are alive
here look: the poet sits
with some bodies considerably
older. There is a blue tinge
of joy in the air
can you all feel it
no. But that's why it is
there. Can you fuckers
reach it. Why do good things
happen. Why does my spine
quiver at the sound of a violin
bow. Why does the dominion
haunt the waking
why write it in pencil
when joy's writ in the air
and you breathe
it disappears
suck in the air of the land
the dingy air those who
made you breathed
and die in a sort of pleasure
and never leave behind
gigantic Christ.

I Will Bring My Mother to the Gates of Heaven

Between modernisms
make souls
crack the skull future
there is a thing for you
there is a bauble dangling
some reticent polemicists
daunt the undulations
but they follow beauty
along the electric lines
into the sodden weeds
bites and tears amongst us
parasites in the rhetoric
blow and burn the dudes
turn the parking lots into
strangers of strange grace
make the lines of your head
gold with tumors brought
through the Christmas of our discontent
display all you can across your
paltry displacement
singe the good into furor
and gods will not be made.
I had two sisters who died
in a fire
I have a brother five years
older than I but
whom I never knew.
My mother tells me this

before she goes away.
I ignore the principal
and I will.
I will bring my mother
to the goddamn gates
of Heaven.

The Orgone Accumulator

The orgone accumulator speaks
in Sanskrit gay marriage has
passed. There is this ancient man
with a shirt and a watch and a
skewed, sickly demeanor
with an orgone accumulator
telling my mother
get in my special box let
my healing energy surge
into your cancerous lungs
into your cavities the doctors
he grins he is so illegal
don't trust oncologists
go up the scales
into the bliss of the
disallowed let the blue
energy clean your sponge
trust me and I will make
you whole. This mad
scientist lives in a nether
place a place where gay
marriage didn't just pass
a place where it doesn't
matter what happens to her
unless it proves his box
his box in the shed.
Let me, the poet, say
this: this started

as a conduit for my love
and rage. This should end
as a recompense
for being for being there
and having done this thing
having let the meat rule
and the TV screen
and the damaging inscription.
We don't know who each others
are. I can luxuriate as I did
in a dream in a heap of dead
squirrels; I can otherwise make
a new vocabulary for this shit
and turn it into blind light
and redemption—for her
for my father for myself
for the song that lasted off
the bottom of our mouths.
All I want is a final love
and the love in between
can the orgone energy
charge a narrative
through these particulars
or are you just a crazy
old and dying man.
Are you just a spark
in a shed
in a town named Suffern.
When you ride New Jersey
Transit into New York
you go through so many towns
with idiosyncratic names

and you think I am gay
and alive in my grief
bring me to Babylon
make a purity out of these
misapprehensions that sold.
Reich if I find you
I will bury your bones in
the swamp of chemotherapy.

July

Bleed not for you, constituents
address the misdirection plains
dig into the grit of ha ha ha
misspell the health insurance
bring the sun closer to the thing
bring the real thing into a teeth
make a jaw of the worst sentence
tell the Jews to finally turn out
and the gays in their misbehavior
to become citizens of a fine death
and sew it all apart with blood
for blood is the root of it
the thing we can't swim around
I love you my mother
I displease my father
all I have are my ditty words
and my supine curses
and the pronouns' fault
sup it up into a goddamn joy
I don't care how many times
I use that word
to scrape a space in June
and call it its own lil' thing
with a Buffalo lilt
the problems that have been had
before are an opportunity
to experience lastly and for real
my mother looked as beautiful

like a figure of myth and dissonance
before she knew what she was for
at least she happened
at least the government
spun itself hegemonic
around my drunken vase
and the light diffused
through my cancer
and I kissed you
and I married boys
nothing is an accident
nothing is a blackness
and an awesomeness that
trails us into beyond
out of this dreaded June
the enemy month
of such displeasure and wan
greatness to follow to
follow the waywardness
into a mud ugly and soulful
July.

My G-d

God do something or not
just make the world swirl
and go about its anarchy
and I will wait impatient
for the peach of your son
in the solar system caring
naught for the petty and a
deranged measurement we
hold to this thing and it will
and it wills that's all we can.

June Ashamed

When I am like this art
just punctures me; familial
concerns remain
wrapped in the polite gauze
of shame
am I ashamed of death
am I ashamed of having
been? There is this thing
a dog we had when we were
healthy now she is sick
deaf and nearly blind
she mewls in the yard
pisses on the couch
and the family talks
in a bastard tongue halfway
between forgone noise
and cable television
will we find our own voice
is that what I, despite money,
want to sing? I think so for
her not for her sake
just into her soul. Let it.

Otto Weidt

Robert Snyderman
writes on a postcard:
This man ran a small workshop
making brushes out of horse
hair and wood employing
the blind, the deaf, and Jews
during the Nazi regime
he himself was
almost totally blind
he hid Jews
in a back room
and followed a Jewess
to Auschwitz where
he arranged her release
somehow
I'm now sitting on the ground
in West Berlin.
My wishes.
(The June heat
beyond intractable
brings as sweat willows
down the face of the mountain.)

Again in June

I will kick in the pants the ambiguous
God who lets my mother stew
in her dying unrest
by loving boys and
making love to boys
again.

Before Breakfast

Hi, I care about you June
talk it out talk
it out
here is what I have
to say to everybody
who lives
I liked it
material
there is a thing in the life
we like to call called mother
fucker. When is my future
I am from the country
silly symphonies
OK just push me
I will put up my dynamite
and do something pretty
with it
I will go all Bugs Bunny
in my leathery bolster
the little girls turn green
bleed out when I cut their
magazines
kiss my chemotherapy
I do more fucked up shit before breakfast
than you've ever dared or dreamed.

Mean Ecstasy

I never knew shit
but was pretty angry
listen to music
the rest of it
kind of is already
mom will die
the things you want
collapse upon themselves
nobody gives you reward
for being honest
the thing keeps
the world keeps selling
so what
so there it is
the verse isn't helping
like it or don't
the reason it does
is so sour and wrong
you must be deranged
with drink and mean ecstasy
to give it for one second
of learning.
Ruin me
never justify.

Money

Sheer mirror.
Money
gets in the way
of me
pulling the eyes out of your soul.

A Tree

The cops showed up
glittering like Christmas
tree snow
and the peasantry
shone in the trickle
of a steady
compulsion
that tumescent
gave you what you
already had.
June is a tree
that grows out
of my rectitude
like a knife.

June Bird

The bird alights on the branch
of an acrimonious tree
and lights a menthol cigarette
June is a crucible
the color of discontinued
cleaning products
the smell of asbestos on fire;
languish incipient
in the fenny detention
of June after
friends scatter
across Europe to marginalize
and a very petite house
melts like a wedding cake
under the cochineal
stained atmosphere;
nothing but a flickering
half-remembered embarrassment
trapped with us inside the
large donut shaped machine
condescending our desperate
attachments
as the schedule runs
headlong into oblivion;
there's really no holding out
for one perspicuous instant
the duration of a book falling
in a burning library

when as by a wipe
the Charybdis spreads wide open
and we are looking down
into the throat of mayhem
the genesis of this diaspora;
no there is no access
there is nothing much to say
or to be done
art fails infinitely
experience suffocates
inside its own packaging
a bird swallows a piece
of glass on a nice day at
the beach we look up
at the sun superstitiously
and say the rote prayers
retiring finally to the
political bedroom;
close the drapes
dissolve into the mattress
as quietly and alone
as forecasting the next year.
I am but as the cuckoo is in June:
heard, not regarded.

The End of June

All the chary roadside wrecks
in the United States of America
seasoned this a delirious June
whither respite done daemonic
puffed up naughty flowerings
what was primarily thought a
cloud determines the edging
off of a progressive company
when a man and his boyfriend
love each other very much he
abuses his inherent sex takes
the object of his affections and
plummets off a haughty surface
that is the way we've all lived
for generations and dagnabbit
nothing's going to stop us now
as now as always I find myself
in another predictable scenario
girlish poetry pervs round itself
chancing over tableaus whereat
a sculptural life of some figurine
brings me to justice that I might
take the face the way his shape
skeletons into my unlikelihood
for I cringe with self-recognition
I am so June for a new stranger
a paragon of boys swaying up
the corner of a stinky old club

the way his eyes burst back to
themselves as if involving seas
in their insouciance and drama
celebrating underage birthdays
a negative century of rad youth
poems can't press up against it
can't or won't reregulate breath
transmogrify into baser instinct
that cream drooling off of flesh
turned out the color of whipped
butter in blustering sightedness
turning upside right inside his
hipster stationary feeling up a
semi-expensive haircut groans
disturb the awed entablatures
shake a semi-valance braining
out of the vortex of the give me
you dancing you unmentionable
are the perfect play on my June
the apogee of my mistimed lust
back to the future to the nestling
ache back away from apt fission
the wronged ex-boyfriends those
spurious phone calls from booths
in the dank wilderness not morn
not yet sun nor an exhilarant turf
away back away from my mouth
which closes and gums upon its
cheap treasure away from grace
upon the wilted and my funereal
grasping away from sordid bliss
hysterically pedantic languages

circling like a wolverine around
monolithic integrity disprizing
a house tousled all carpet ready
made June's prognosis engaged
to sick desperation in silly acts
it's enough because it makes a
mind reel for you are enough for
a thousand summer days I feel
and here I don't even know you
nor ever will I whatever age we
accident into having washed off
our impatient and brutal luxury
like wars and admirable hygiene
I wrote away from you writing
rent a certain obsession for my
own commercial torment get in
the van and drive so far afield it
hurts meanwhile it is said there
is a summer home on a sloping
green where a woman feels her
cancer through a hushed veil of
medicine and tolerance in June
the pretty boy turns so red in the
disco light and fades out like the
broke television turning off slow
these plateaus meander crazily
everything is murder nothing to
out nothing to stare in the faces
of if God can be said to have so
many faces rather than a team
of litigious anachronisms dealt
out in service of blinding error

I can't get our old boy band back
together nor can my upset mom
turn against an ugly hometown
extremis or body woe or bodies
fallen in closer battles from the
countries of quotidian malaise
woe is he who is a June in army
he who dares to take his arms
off in a pitch colored sanctuary
plastering his little time around
a harried due slunk forth until
the worst is just until spinning
fractures top the horny defeat
besides every night I made my
bed and cradled a bottle of ale
in the crease of my elbow and
there and in that mood wrote
out a malodorous registration
and certain milky ballots for
my comfort or its ownership
till exhausted I set down my
quill and called the land line
in Lakewood, New York and
listened to her terminal songs
that left me heartsick and drunk
looking for a nicety in dearth
masturbating into the clothes
I wore for a fortnight and let
my prurient boy use without
express permission to collect
deposits of lukewarm semen
which we should have rightly

hid behind our manumission
afore with unfamiliar interim
authority I filed punk histories
in the vault I put my mother's
name across for a tenderness
and as a part of my living will
in case I die before my own id
in case a gay firmament starts
out toward some better galaxy
where poems get put to sleep
like rabid dogs and poets are
subjects of genocide for their
lofty but condemned desires
this is proven and supported
as is the failure and the glory
reneged while I forge my rest
by damn and under high noon
enough devouring entitled June
how now to then an end in June
outsourcing pat to make room
for mortality moreover for the
preceding anxiety shame and
fear until I have nothing to say
in months because having lost
a sense of anything I am happy
to at least be able to dream of
you alive.

Crush Dream

All Good Years

In the year 1993 in the municipal parking lot
a hapless woman collapsed against her car
and her earring fell off and she knelt on it
the sun was white and the roof was flat
and something evil happened in her skull
where her spine pierced her brain toylike
similarly near the end of the millennium
in the city an uncle the family disavowed
emaciated in a narrow bed with tubes in him
opened his mouth as his lungs filled with blood
and the black nurse put down her magazine
in the year 2009 the man with the truck howled
into the chest of some haphazard off-duty cop
near the drive-thru lane at a local restaurant
after unwittingly backing over a baby stroller
with a four week old newborn girl in it that
a mother had left unattended for only a second
and later in the year that the world ended (2012)
on the exact sites of provincial freak accidents
where the quotidian and unappreciated loss
drooled out of the chronology of petty histories
burnished fountains sprung from within the earth
and shot where years magnify into a heaven
and god leaned out the passenger-side window
of his brand new decked-out luxury vehicle
on the empyrean interstate in time to wink
at the sputtering faucets reaching up jealously
toward something I know that I will carry
but fear that I will never learn how to say.

Crush Dream

I am the little Dutch boy
in the branch of a linden tree
Nobody loves me   I am
so lonely.

Give Love Away but Charge for the Verse

Multiple linguists have famously positioned
themselves across the small part of town
where the staff puts a difference in my hair.
I am not quite able, not quite feeling, sir
I am not telling the truth for the hell of it
I am not even though, I am not the song
you purchased   but I'm the song
you get.
When my peers saw my ashen dimensions
occasionally one of them pitifully sulked
into a daring smile, spilt wild milk follows
and darned the portrait of a graceful pass.
Harrow
and bemuse.
There are only barren lands
and topsy curves
and one night stands;
there are only the things you invest in my
genius.   There are only the ways to
God and man, to wallows work and session
bands, to bankruptcy and to the fallow urges.
I knew a man named Richard who
drove a car into my room
and told me not to watch my dealerships.
But it was too late, I fear, for all of that
for misery, mise-en-scène, and dastard
flat, for derring-do or hunger or a cure.
For I have lived a million days if I have

lived a year, I'm sure.   And none
the wiser, none the better for it. So shit.
Several different excuses have occurred
to the turn key this quarter. We await
instead of aspiring. I will compensate
for that, you shall parse all obligatory
relegations in the tree of my odd youth.
God is a factory, God is above.
I am a victory I
am a love.
Pay me.

Time

I have done
myself
a favor
in
the last
several minutes.
The only thing
I've eaten
in
the last
two days
is
a boy's ass.
Here
I almost
ashed
in
my water glass.

Crushed Perfume

The young man told me that when he
gets aggressive his vision blurs elaborating
September making the randomness behind
the tiny wars of feign in his reflexes twitch like
an embarrassed classicism and in that wont
the fingers of love untangle and he floats off
into space and intercourse.
Do you remember tracing paper?
I put it on the windows of all my sets
back when I had sets back when
I had lights to shine through them.
Doctor Faustus lights the lights but
all I do is hide from eventual debt.
You are better than this, once an angry man
told me. But when I got around to being
better than this, everything around me had
died and I had died and the century was ruined
and did you know that you were born with curt
redemptions? Did you ha ha know that blah
blah? When I listen to Conrad I feel like fear
has given birth to a diamond inside of my colon
and I feel like I broke into my friend's apartment
and masturbated on his furniture and wrecked a
bottle of his perfume in my impermissible palm
and let the pristine shards cut my skin as the
thematic scent bled in, into my body not into
my soul and into baptism not into the goal.

Do you know, tired withstand, know
what crushed perfume smells like
to a desperate hand?

Adjectives

What was open about your ingress
in the lick of our intolerant hour
at the bottom of a juvenile meer
toward the purpose of impractical
and desultory imaginings of truth
and love?
I look into your argent tooth
and wait for the mouth
to close again.

Alive

The world does not permit anyone to die
just to become irrelevant to the immortal living
because money does not die and because
we worship and want to live in the image
of money we believe we shall not perish
from this painful version of life. Those who
have seen death are duly suppressed
and our grief becomes embarrassing
and void and we become a problem.
When there's no skull in the standing
of my choler and there's no mother
in the neck of my assays any longer
I will peel away the awarded and monied
and live as a force for the person I should
be no matter how unimportant or unsustainable
he is.

Valentine's Day

Monster from the planet of blood
you and everything you hear
I sit sullenly in the armory listening
to my lover's hair
               go to hell
young gangsters, existing, a windowsill
he put his hot mouth in her last days she said
could I could any of it I wanted to bury
you in loquacious guilt and if I had thanked
a thousand girls in prison and if I had seen
a friend tattooed in her own remorses I was
and am still useless and around
but I no longer have good intentions
for any boy in the universe
Ryan is bothering me while I'm trying
to finish this poem he says
"It's not too late to change your mind
                 and go to heaven
SAVE YOURSELF."

Dream Date

O fuck you
I can still
taste you therefore
you still
are real.

The Night Attempt

Frowningly out of the suburban dark an inconsequential blade
of silvered light sliced horizontally across the access road
and curled around with Methodist angst the forgiven lamps
that hung dry and disabused from consistently asinine stations
but the glow was denied an entrance to the bulbs and shivered
shirking back to the lovely hell it came from and the hamlet
naughtily and unaware remained crowded in its discontent
till again the planet lurched back to the pale and dewey norm.

Sacred Franchises

Everybody died
in the white
of your make-up.
I set forth
to be beholden
to the horror
of my sacred franchises.
There is a gold
statue of me
hanging in the sky
over the Kremlin.
You took egregious birds
inside the pink cost
the sun went down
kids earned regretfully
and before they knew
it they were prostrate
and weeping bankrupt.
I became a stomach
in which the tell
forgot itself.
And love is encompassed
in dark animals
all that I wanted I forgot
and boded late as
a minion of
my definition:
technologic,

sore,
protruding.
Till an ending or
till you.

No

What crushes me, like the weight of God, dinosauring
blank space into my throat, what cannot be unless
I believe in it, is one of the only things I care
to think about. Hammer
without a name, clavicle of my resorts, be a matter
and a bill, withstand the damages of a graphic aria
with no form but an insatiable form, no justice
but an intelligence, no grade. Indolence,
December it, unreliable take it into the violent attic
to darn and husk and wash and sew and betroth
casual nevers and say, turned castrated out of social
authority, use your words, mannequin.
     They put you on the cheapest bus
     and drove sidelong into indemnity.
     Some day I will accept this; till then
          you will just allow me.

Food Stamps

Government!
Your tiny bat face puckers
through defaulting and insolvent chambers;
thanks for the free money
I used to buy cigarettes and Ballantine
before getting a guy over here
to fuck on a swan.
Don't tread on me,
I'm covered in silicone-based lube.

Your Burning House

If you have me, you are trying to sit down forever.
Clint Eastwood is Popular Culture; God just wants
to live His life. Isn't it funny when somebody says,
"It's always the last place you look"? Of course it is,
why would you keep looking after you've found it?
I could move to Canada and still be an American.
Business first, pleasure afterwards; this will end
in tears. Happy birthday, dear everybody, the room
is so quiet I can hear myself swallowing coffee.
Kill me. Mom's arm grew back smaller but, hey,
what can you do? I can't sort them out, I can't
live on bread and cigarettes, sloppiness. I have
yet to become a great poet. Parts of the midwest
are completely uninhabitable, according to my sister.
This is probably just a teaching moment, extreme
talent, almost beyond belief, bleeding out of a swan's
ear in Brugge. I don't need you, I don't want you,
the light so light it floats, the hardly painful offering,
little girls who toss themselves into the spring.
I'm really really in love; not much else to report.
What would you tell me if we were in the room
alone together, what would you save from
your burning house?

The Devil Is in the Woods

What is this machine, to which Magnolia tree
does humiliation trailer as everything saying to
alter, where actress does the body, whence
from elaborating streams of oblivious gallants
falter, scrambling deafness in the reach, being
as a broken leaf stubbed into a lusty market,
whining? The position of almond turns breathes
in chosen proximities to characters out of the
drift, don't abound on broad forgiven aspects.
The lamb is choking on her metaphor, god is
masturbating to his high school yearbook, and
the devil is in the woods.

The Future

First we crushed into each other in a blue room
a carafe of your carelessness sates me for a year
I am the star of my own truncated privacy, love-
less and harrumphing, see you soon ridden mass
...or else!

Love Poem

You are the only
outside of the provinces
and beside grammar
"Why do you only say 'love' in poems?"
I made the imaginary voice say
and time, get him talking about it
and before you know it
you are somehow famous inside
of the darkness of your
ordering, if that makes any sense
listen
I LOVE YOU
my dead mother
my lovers
and my friends
in poems I try to squirm about the
spaces between the objects
the objects in the thoughts
the holy kisses
the true beast diminishes
I am drunk and I am listening to music
and I LOVE YOU
take that for what it is not worth
buy me a new life
so that I might save the hell from you
time, get
get in my carelessness
I have used these words before

and somewhere in the century
she exists
and
of the
somewhere in my life
a dog is crying to death.

A Swan

I closed myself into the florid word
and talked out of defiance for a swan
in my dreams our love makes sense
and the un-awarded car that drives us
how can I be so gentle with myself
chat with perfidy long distance, scout
burn into your ignoble intentions
the slowing loveliness of a noted mom
and make your way away into a glom.
There was a poem in there somewhere
I was sure before I lay down to write.

All Gentlemen

I kissed you on your brow so you would not
grow another year, have you not heard them
or their deafening conglomerates I shall not
witness another tragedy so simple and benign
that would insert me into the Berlin of cause
that would round lives outside of the nearest
text would you be my one and only would I
be the best for you? I didn't think so either so
here we are gentlemen all superlative in the
taste of unconsecrated dimensions proving
or so we think ourselves outside of science
and the touch of relevancy in contamination
when the hell was it so base, when did god
walk outside of the bower of his daft face?
When was I supposed to place a dainty tea
cup in the displaced lap of lapsing tolerant
and the considerations of it if it please you
$\qquad$ all gentlemen?

Quiet Leviathan

Emotions are unsuitable, which is why they work.
What do I pray for in my pillaging when the end
of the day emerges from my cold and distilled face.
I must not trust words, that must be the thing
the gym inside a kind of unsounded trumpet that
I just let lie crass and submissive in my act as I
drown in the salt lake of tremendous plagiarism.
To use the words, to solve my egoistic calumny
meaning the time it takes me to get up of mornings
and put on my specs. O, godlike disaster, there is
hardly any human cleverness to rectify the price.
There is only the image of what I want to be done
and have existed, throbbing in the memory of what
prideful I dare not speak and what educated in the
embarrassing language of self I can't make a tune to.

Urgent Precision Ass

Die, devices and disorder
disclosure, adamant infantile
wear a default english
tush avarice, butt sometimes
when a man has reached his age
the golden door shall whale
idyllic, come write with us.
Half of the world population
doesn't know who the other
half is.

Wholly Aware Are We

We are the same living as we are dying.
Be careful in both respects, respondent.
The time has come to dispense egalitarian
horses across the ghosts of our high school
selves. Your mother was once beautiful
and had fields of willingness spreading
out in sorry flowers across her sheets.
She had the basic money, spent it well.
When she passed, the passenger of her
wonder turned into an intolerant frieze
that whispered along the minor keys.
Be careful of what I am in a breathing
all who sign malevolent contracts fail.
The shelf life of your remembering will
trace my love for miles along the plane.
Service, who we wholly are aware.

Every Poem I Write Is an Accident and Remember You Are Going To Die

Simple
      but perfect
            the wayward
the face of it is as ugly
you won't
          you will
make fun of me
      I am
sincere.

A Beautiful Room

Dear Edmund, the things
mimesis portrays about
the things themselves
brightens and imbues
      the things
with a gorgeousness
we hardly deserve
unless we put our souls
to the floor of the hauteur
of the heart of god
      herself.
Edmund, there is a black
room filled with ruined columns
where I dwell with you in
place twixt rapture and grace
      and
death and disaster
there is a life there for us in
my feckless imagination
      and I call it
      Philadelphia.

Liminal Spacing

Here, in my hand, is a dream I have kept
kissed in the clench of said hand;
I let my grasp slack a little and the
dream breathes like vacations themselves.
My life takes place in a dreamer's awkward
shrugging in the sideways pseudo-modernism
of an airport lounge. I can't say that
I love it, it's just what is happening.
The flight is never really coming;
the anticipation is all. I don't really
know how to say these things, they
linger in the yellow jaw of an oblique
Russian alligator. When I try to put
it to verse... just... jingles... just erred
slogans result. God! I can say
in the future: I will love for true!
I can say this, say... naked and nearly
weeping with bizarre, horny shame
on top of the filthy bedspread
in a smoking room of the nearest
Motel 6, masturbating repeatedly and
dreaming of you... the past... the time
we turned a similar room into our
last vacation. And I belonged to you
in Denver. I am never going to make it
to Chicago. I am never going to move
to California. I can feel the closeness
of the breeze of the thing that would

make this real. I am never going to see...
God! what a disgraced bias coincides
with the course of the lives
when you look at it.

A Tiny Fluffy Puppy

I must dedicate this much
of my brain
to being socially/
economically retarded
or else there's no way
I could, you know,
make art;
a tiny fluffy
puppy barks at and challenges
a piece of broccoli lying on the floor.

Buena Vista Park

Be eloquent, dismembering the music that
situated us. Be prurient, run up the fronts
the sexy diagonals of Buena Vista park.
Dream of a sloping alley carpeted with
condoms, the leaves turning inward toward
the sex at the bottom of my heart. Look
at the chalky city, alabaster ruins of the
present itself, searing daringly, unabashed
in the idle shine. Tusk-charred groupings
stuck preciously out of the brown ground
moving low up toward the blistered hues
from god. The seedy verdancy encroaches
yawning into my bleached-out mirror
kisses me upon my spotty cheek.
I am of no class, I am in the woods
where deviants cruise, where dogs
chew each other's throats out in
California, a land of wears and wires
that goes to sleep early, while I
climb a church tower and plot.
You are orange in your memory, O
land, and fermented with the blood
of sovereign crying. The normal
crying, that we do at home
and the tears creaked out from
the ugly stars we see at night
that hit our heads, parked

as we are, in the good view
at the summit
of a tall hill.

Friend Song

O my friends
take coverage
under the unsaid
verbiage
O my friends
be my friends
in an extracurricular
space
accidents provided
O my friends
be we where
I found you there
in the ignominy
and the shriek
of better days
we have lived
but never knew
my friends
be there.

Personal Poem

I am severally dangerous only
to myself but in crowds
introverted as I am
repugnant in my grief
of self I will
decimate a few social
situations just
to learn that anyone
cares to listen
to such expression.
          Also I'm an alcoholic.

You're the Top

You're the top
I'm the whore and the holy one.

You're adroit
I'm a stick of chewing gum.

You're insane
I'm Helen Keller.

You're Frank O'Hara
I'm getting better.

You're arrested
I'm an expensive college degree.

You're the top
I'm the massacre at Wounded Knee.

We do not get along very well together
you and me do we?

I'm Sorry

A boy in an off-the-rack suit
waist deep in a lurid pond
hands in his pockets and
staring at a swan
swimming on the surface
of the water the tawny color
of the winter sky.

Waiting for a Young Man

Thou art a grass map of my wanting
       narrative equals death
I sit and wait   again
there shall be small strings
that cling between his face
(no touches of disaster upon it)
and the rallying spirit I suppress with
       drink
           mere drink and *gossip*
waiting for a young man in
the station house
possibly conceived and done without
       sex is evil, sex is sublime
a young man has no concept of time
or what I could do   to him
or what projections I'll impose upon
his glassy wink
and the calm field of soft hairs
speckled across his twiggy forearm
       how does it feel when I touch it?
"What are you thinking?"
       How to save you from me
       and me from myself
to put it in the simple style
           of thy kiss.

Home Sweet Home

Hapless lay the oranges and harmless
clucks the swan
I've swallowed meager enchantments
ignoring all the governing signals
I've been drawn here before
in the dank gym sock smell
of this particular discotheque
the crushing incidental basement
a fragmented and disingenuous light
incentivizes me from the bottom of
my glass
gaze don't shirk but glower
admiring the symmetry of our bodies
thrusting into each other half clothed
underneath the damning florescent yawn
squeaking across the ammonia stained tiles
of the women's bathroom
stomach like a dream I put under my boot
mouth like a crater of solution
searching inside the boy for my own grief
turning him around in the light like a prism
fade out
fade in
try again.

One Day and a Night in Baton Rouge

If you have to go out and do something
till the Pleiades internet themselves to marl
then somebody is going to drunkenly scrawl
"faggot" across your locker, scream "fuck
you!" from a swerving car in Baton Rouge.
If you have to be so very contemporary
till your fawning underexposure is tenured
then I am going to fuck your wife, writing
"faggot" in lipstick across her twat till
you renege into your unemotional abashment.
If you have me
till I smile
then I will be your
"faggot" in Baton Rouge and
you will be one day and a night.

Even the Most Extreme Consciousness of Doom Threatens to Degenerate into Idle Chatter

Any shock there is has not done
me in enough
for all offers die in themselves
if you like me you will give me money
and I shall live for myself
and my leafy grief and my paranoia
my hatred of the body or
economy
I just want a dick in me
I suppose, or the other way round
as if it matters at this point
play chess inside the poetry
but may I say that I have seen
the person I most love in life
turn hairless, green, and die
in front of my eyes
and, as Adorno says:
To write poetry after Auschwitz is barbaric
        every single suburban end
the synecdoche of a continuing soul-genocide.
(What has happened and what
has yet to
are the same
thing...)

Duly

We used to be better put together
and one day it might be again.
Turn around inside of a dark groom
pasture everything, and here I thought
you loved me.
Really what I thought what I was doing was
pulling a swan into controversial abstinence.
Belie me while I prepare
to talk about what I have to say.

Restraint

Random
truck,
fan fiction,
death &
disaster;
series weep
in the circle
of dirt
in the backyard
where
the pool used
to be.

Be a Good Girl

I have no idea
if you will ever find these words
but god I want you to,

Answered Prayers

I swear I will be still
I should think
to watch
a comfortable, haunted man
I will ruin my life
drown my book
end the palace
of my diamond vantages
with a special recusal
from my
desire of sequence
anything in the orange light
of my word for you
anything
to excuse
all the pain.

Violence

       I found it
walking normally
wanting English
going back to
the understood help
    matter this is
a tart poise to keep
                swan
into an ash   harm
into a series of continued
reprisals.
We do not negotiate
      with terrorists.
If I had children, I would
protect   them.
      (Answer.)

Check Your Watch

If you knew what was going on in here
the long salve would bunk itself to be
grown, the arm inside a single hooking
startling me awake previously where is
the love type doing, work up the wrong
and realize
every single moment on a trauma check
your watch.

Smoker's Corner

I'll meet you in smoker's corner
in the yellow brush at the edge of the
yard
wearing a tasseled wig
puling
and seriously scared
who are you?
when I take my smeary glasses off
all I see are darling shapes
you can judge me
and fall in love with my sickness
all the small slopes of the middle school
that long left me with animal guilt
told me that when we grow up
everything will crush
we will find hospitals of ourselves
darkened and bereft in our
heavenly insurances
if I could write a poem that sang
out the awkwardness
expelled the loss
in a smoke ring
like a bad kid out of home room to
expunge the briefness bodily
and lung myself to you
then I would know enough truth
to last me till my blood dries up.

Six Absences

1. The changing of the yards, blithely, schemers
taunt the infrastructure of each other's friendships
dark insertions, no longer can they be named.

2. Petty alcoholisms, turned out to the right bench
waters of the passenger, crushed dreams of a new
fall, understand me, for I cover my own hatred.

3. Unspoken experience that makes me doubt the
abilities of verse, things I keep to myself, what is
hardly translatable not even to myself in poetry.

4. Hard love, but more likely the gift to believe
that the whole mythos is shattered and I've grown
out of myself and should just anonymously die.

5. The dynamics of a whipped shadow cursing all
homes in the wrecked hill of my supposed quality
spreading without a name, doing another still thing.

6. How never does a kiss remind me of your death
truthfully, I just want to slaughter all of the god
and am here so frightened I cannot even write it.

Negative Accomplishments

If I talk about myself enough I will drive all the way into you.
I think I will take a ludicrous sabbatical
(the sacred harp)
Near-constant
(   )
really gets
to you.

To Loosen the Hand and Have Mercy

And there is within me a jointed denial
to be present in this alleged story, prayer
to be free in the better mind repeating it
guzzle a ton of marked notes deservedly
a voice on the phone with porous news
which I would rather stray from proving

Not knowing what the matter is, revolt
against your agency not loving whatever
comes to this, take your default gracefully
born for field and thunder over the brain
I wonder if I could ugly heavens strain
upon the sight of my mom's last breath

Songs of power and discord have reached
me in my stupor, you are a dream I crush
between my sibilant toes and the carpet
when I have no more joys for the weight
of late capitalism and a good john who
cares as much about the rise as the fall

Go for what till the church is up with blood
I can head for it if you look under my hood
take my hand, grey weaver, and disappear
we all shall weep for what has been a year
destroyed in the acrimony of a selfishness
torn through without relief or common bliss

The verse was fucked to start with though
I would have reached my heinous retreat
if all eschewing and murderous I could
thoughts damn by longing and obliquity
but I would rather save my unearned soul
God, to loosen the hand and have mercy!

Acceptance

If I can't bring my voice up toward
a tacit god, if beauty can't be wrought
from experience, then it is not worth
it, it is a gilt limb smooching and
refusing the word.
There is a continuum with two
poles, dumb
confession and dumb language, and
strung hidden between is
the truth.

Happy Birthday

Miles out of the way I came upon a short woman
who, on my birthday, was already weeping
she blocked the path and didn't care she
put her miniature hand upon my chest, looked up
then, with damning gaze, said she
"You are in tremendous pain, I mean physical pain
and you have no idea where it is coming from
and you have no idea how to make it stop."

Challenger

Something Happened

I saw a black cat with a chicken bone in her mouth.
The time has finally come in my life to make difficult choices;
when my mother died, no difficult choices were made
it just happened
I watched her die on a Hospice bed in the living room
and as my father turned orange and cried
I stood up and turned off the television
which was playing a rerun of CSI: Miami.
I wake up into a future that I have spent
the last seven years buying out.
When my mother died she did not look at peace
her jaw was open slack revealing her teeth and pale tongue.
The mortician came in a black suit and dressed her
I was asked if I wanted a final moment with the body.
That whole week was so terrible, honestly we
were relieved it was over, the suffering and all.
Before she wasn't able to get upstairs anymore
I found her on my way to the guest room
in the middle of the night, slumped halfway out of bed
just collapsed into her own lap
(the lights were on but her exhausted husband slept)
I semi-drunkenly approached her and pulled her shoulders up
and laid her back horizontally on the mattress
I whispered, "I love you"
and she moaned through the drugs, "I love you."
I wish I could say that was the last exchange
but she later chastised me for smelling like cigarettes
and told me she was worried about my survival

and that was the real last thing she said to me
or really at all, except she could say "No."
Dad: "Do you want some water?"
Mom: "No."
Anyway, I resented her lack of faith in my life
as expressed in a sedative haze through her pain
but it's becoming increasingly clear her worries
were honest, practical, and very founded;
I am apparently an adult and have absolutely no way to exist.
I hate money, I hate it, and I hate myself.
Love means less and less every day we are alive.
Love is good but it's not going to save us
or keep the lights on.
My boyfriend fucked me tonight without a condom
or lubricant; my anal wall started bleeding and
he cut open his dick before he came
and I shit blood
and he poured hydrogen peroxide on his dick
and we both felt stupid, stupid and like crying.
That is an example of something
that doesn't belong in a poem
but at this point, you know, *fuck it.*
Every day I wake up a little less of a lie
and a little more destroyed in my citizenship
and I've never been more terrified.

The Sacred Harp

There is a place between the ax and earth
to challenge the validity of breath
the soft-spoken explosion in our love.
My better self, a series of cold days
slowly defamed all took and burned away
mildewed corners in the bathroom of night.

I Don't Care to Stay Here Long

A wonder what is place in understood
devotion to a tricky relapsing
to speak around the curse of human life
and put a name toward the debutante
who, cyclical, enjoys the eaten plain.
If I could say something so personal
to be broadcast across my wherewithal
then presidents would stand down in their shame
and we would be justified to our names
and all the tickling ghosts would jettison.

I will stave off my currency
deranged
abjured into a better galaxy.

New Verlaine

A gaudy supposition decided
that grief would be discovered in pale yards
and we could leave a desperate trace across
the surface of the house's living room.
Coward, it's but a drill inside my brain
and yet one day a sated grace shall rise
we will fly into a land of deep shade
if there's a time un-pierced by human thought
if I can work backwards from the cancer
into pictures fulfilled by hapless love
pictures that never did exist in full.
So this is all my fault, it is my fault.
The white people, they died in the ocean
they died in the hospitals on the earth
their humor died in the want of money
they tucked away their empathy falsely
they bought into perverse securities.

I can't say what it is I think I've done
I'm far too irresponsible for that
hour was I stood beneath weeping angels
attached to my declamations or what
a misinterpreted Rimbaud would see
spread swarding over slopes of youthful piss
until I begged home, overwrought and sick
looking for a new Verlaine to save me.

An Empty Room

I don't want to go home I
want to be simple.
My failures betray a benign rebus
crying out in some campy parking lot
that looks over a store that
has gone bankrupt.

Art is the Commodity

I challenge you to a duel of sluts
mourning stupidly in daft bastions
vomiting pronouns and assumptions
putting strange objects in its vagina
I came to this country full of lice and mania
laid up in Ellis Island's hospital
a tumor grown upon poetic eyes
the Internet knows what it's like
finally things unchallenged
in the putrid faze of change
the government owns every ugly part of me
fundamental petards disposed
to a lot of gay fun.

Two Bridge

It's cold outside and every bird is chirping
like euphemisms pressed against the dawn
the bridge of remembering and the bridge
of never quite getting there again
make two bridge.
If this had been an invented thing
or part of a luxurious descent
the white dog would have parted
before the white dog returned.
(Are you going around with that rough guy?)
It takes reading
to realize
the worst

the body is your party.

Poem for Klaus Nomi

At my mother's death bed I sat
with her priest
who told me
how nice it was I am creative
because it's so seldom, she said
that you see young talent
and I said
there was a generation of great minds
but they
all died in the 80's
and she blinked and she said
yes, that's what they say, isn't it?

I am up against a surface
never to be lonely
crawling out of myself I
guess I care too much
their long hair and their faces
it all kind of hung together
till we had so far of it
there is a darkness in the past.

(He thought Penicillin would be
a cure for all and
pop it before you go to the trucks.)

Over the frontiers
of the war interpretation:

If I saw your face could you still
take a bow
would we know you know you
know you by now?

The lunar eclipse...
Float
I just can't help it.

About the Marriage of Amour and Psyche

for Adrian & Sweeney

I.

The golden tropes of America are
(like deranged angels) swirling round our heads
on the drive to work, the dentist, friends
in this diaphanous, rote, and merry
bubblegum circumspection
that all our unctuous wards are the heirs to
—to soap, to yearn without essential bob
till when in a fork's devised: the rowdy
secession, revolt in honor's due
then the breath pauses before you
and we sing into a thousand flaming skies
abrupt, serenely damaged, in disguise
my lungs are carried to you on the wind
through a city that hasn't yet begun.

II.

Conjure through the technologic aspect:
no newspaper clipping will be the same
a holy writ thus intertwined in name
with the tandem thirsts of love and faith
just as two souls mature, actualize
at their joint, preternatural urgings
so that one's desire, and need, for the other

is the instigating magic
that calls the complimented (and complicit)
desire for union into life
and the variegated solstice rises
and lends itself unto the sacred harp!

A dual existence is as base as
the cotton that winds in earthful gyre
and it is as blessed yet as effaced as
an intellect that scribes "Universe"
—like motion, indelible cursive—
between the heart and where you put your hand
(basins bled out into un-supporting
habitats we'd wrestled by destination
and surfaced like twin gobbets on the sun)
as burns, as burns, the mortal fire.

III.

Time was, time is, and time will be again
like title brings allegiance to the crest
come forth, all gentle acolytes
wring close within the gates of fond record
as we'll be fulfilled—shining in the rest
(For we are nothing but promises; girls
who stir inside unanimous valleys
for whom fact accomplished melts, slugs adrift
because our discourse, our contracted brush
brings the hysteric moon to *where you are*
suspended in delicious memory
from whence come, what nurtured the pilgrimage
now new futures pass daily through our lips).

You won't return to familiar office
as this brandished and designed scripture
co-mingles, wizardly, with the impress
of a shoulder-touched meadow of renewal
—the kids are probably alive
meant for rare hens, truck and peacetime (rejoice)
which is a form for all of those who broke
a tanned and elder page from lovely crafts
and all of those who are, resolved, composed
inside of a perfect spindle of truth.

Telephones and radios, replete
with important announcements of the cause
reverberate in the place between the skulls
and if she has nothing but his just breast
and he nothing but her theologies
of distances spanned and time depressed
then, love-earned, endear that gift to me
and forever, succinct in each other
wed out deliveries into the world
and exist, priceless collaboration—*exist!*

I Belong to the Dark Cinema

There's a naked girl in the lens of my farthest
I am writing away from her again
just know that in my heart I am sorry
if I could still be on my feet in this.
I am to the southwest of my deliverance
buy everybody out of the online
while I am still the helpless precedent
shooting a soundless bullet
into your sense of dividends
all I want it to do is give me room.
      And you
if you can't
      I will tell myself
          I will die
             and let you sort it out
      but you won't.

June Rises

She drapes herself amongst the conifers
as we give ourselves into distance
and I flow
like a salt water over trust
        there is a songbird, claws upon her throat.
I think you are all right
I mean, I think you will keep living.

Long Book

Hey, if you have something
I can work around it.

And take me out into the woods and can
I find inside the fire of god, myself?

The signs and borders that have killed my mom
a long time before we listened to her.

There is in the sex
we're in it.

As a woman, politic in her game
I can't tell my living without her death.

Still to the dear table
all of my fucking nights' argot.

I will readily put my feathers on
top of the expiring summer says.

Something to delete
as in also I still of a upon it an will.

It is true that loss does make us deeper
in that it pulls us into nothingness
just an incremental margin further
and in our sense we decimate true bliss.

This will be a long book.

Zachary

Let me cry into your chest
on this sheetless mattress
at least for now
let met and me
forget
meet me
on the long slope
meet me inside
of my constant loss
and occasional grief
that bleeds through my duty to life
from my eyes
into your chest
I did these things
and said what I said
I fell in love with you
after my mother died
the world
retards me
I don't even believe in myself
I might be as worthless
as my father thinks
but this special sort of injury
nurtures itself inside my heart
through pathetic job interviews
and begging for lunch
and this love for you, Zachary
is captured in rarefied moments

infinitely outside of capitalism
when you hold me weeping in
your naked arms
and I hear your heart pulse
and think of my mother's body
dying
and the small hairs on your chest
collect everything.

I Came to Belong to Lazarus

This summer belongs to the devil
and four cancers bemoan insertion
wake up and feel your bones
and read more and love more
and kiss the one you earn.

You asked me what was going on
between god and I, these days?
We're not on speaking terms.

Lazarus was Jesus' boyfriend
who god killed
but Jesus said No
my father's death shall not take him
he will live again
and so the tomb was empty
for some time after that.

Love Is Greed and Then Some

I am a castle
I am a dream
of what is not to come
I wear make-up
I talk
I say Fine
I have something
under my fingernails
I want to know Love
I want to be inside
god is my name
for the blood
blood is my name
what that I breathe
when I think about this
it all is furthermore.
        It all is come.
                You do not worry me
I am the greatest story ever told
to an idiot
on the brink.

        Arboreal
        and furious
        comes death
        to destroy my economy.

My Dad

Sir, I am not ready
but if you knew
sir, if you knew how I loved
and what I loved and wherefore
sir, your bones would turn to dust
and a thousand galaxies, trust
would turn into your dolls
because I hate you inside of economy
and love you outside of my sad duty
I am a creature you dreamt about
in high school
that left your sheets damp, bloodied.

I know my father cannot speak
doctors cut into his vocal chords
I know my father cannot speak
the culture never gave him words
they let him drop bombs
and raise a son
and his son said hallelujah
and he drove him to the airport
after his mom's death.

I am a poet yet
somehow grew naked from my parents.

Space Is Filled with a Billowing Sea of Quantum Particles that Jump in and out of Existence

He fucked me and came
and some come got on the mattress
I ran to get a wet rag
"Why?" he asked
"To clean up this come," I said.
"But a little come never hurt anyone," he said.

"That's not true."
"Yes, you're right," he reconsidered.

> *Why it's Gabriel playing, why it's Gabriel saying*
> *Will you be ready to go when*
> *I blow my horn?*

You are all too full of expensive dinners.

A Year Nearly

Higher falls
the whole enterprise
          as I dream of dying in a storm

There is an art
to a
plummeting boy
dislodging neighboring familiar
for the purposes of proper spelling
and indigenous grammar I sucked off.

It is nearly a year since mother's   death.

Uh-Oh

I have lived
so I felt love.
When the arc was sprung from the mind of her
and the cabin of astronauts went down
like an embarrassed girl on the dance floor
challenging the ocean behind a curl
of slurred debris, the girl's last call was
changed and introspect, a simple "Uh-oh."

Church Problem

In the most progressive house of worship
the assemblywoman cowered anyway
her sympathies petulantly shut
to a band of crusty travelers
wallowing in their piss on the soil
around the graveyard, around the fence.
They scrawled Fuck You in white block letters
with latex paint on the portico's bluestone slate floor
and on a statue of a lion, and on the rose.
Also they said, The eyes and the mouth gnaw; they said
Fuck you Fuck you God like everyone else before!
The poets in the backroom saw this and
alerted the rector; when she came out
she spied three culprits squatted round the portico,
one man, a woman, and something unidentifiable
but they all fled, running past her
(the poets recognized the woman, said they see
her all the time, her golden hair).
The assemblywoman dialed the police on her phone
from the pocket where she lay tousled and lilliputian
behind the coats in the odds-and-ends closet.
"I've called the cops," she mewed, "they're on
their way!" The rector bowed her neck and said
"Let's better get out some turpentine, some steel wool
let's set to work on this mess before it dries..."
The poets took out their cigarettes and dabbled to the yard
gossiping and feeling insecure/profound.
The responding officers took the rector and the poet-witnesses

on a ride around the general area to see if they could spot
the vandals, but they didn't find them in the crowds.
The rector disclosed that the church had received recently
a modest grant to the tune of 100 thousand dollars for the
purpose of minor restorations, which would include
brushing up the historic portico (it'd also entail work
on the whole front area and roof above the entrance).
She said that. It was time to get out of the police
car. Back at the church, three *different* vagabonds
were newly installed by the portico, nodding off
in stinky rags with a rat dancing in the trash
above their shivering, puckered heads.
(The assemblywoman glowered nervously
from the side window overlooking the yard;
when one of her subjects made a sudden move
she flinched out of her pumps and her hair
went spewing into her lipsticked mouth.)
A man wearing a fedora rolled up on a beaten scooter
a sleeping bag strapped to his back from his
shoulders to his ass; by now there was a smattering
of reporters, one of whom addressed the newcomer
inquiring if he knew anything about the graffitiers' crime.
"The woman with the golden hair must of done it," he cawed
"The name's Goldilocks; my name's Tinkerbell. I ain't
got nothing to do with no painting of words and letters
on this portico or anywhere else... but, sure, we all know
Goldilocks. She's not welcome here but she comes
anyway, with her friends. One of them we don't believe
is human. It sucks when they come round, for trouble...
and to yell things and to write angriness about God."
The rector shook her head, vexed. "Why the church?"
she whimpered. "The fuzz jump us in the park now,

take our shoes, beat us with our own hats and shoes
tell us it's past curfew when it's not even dusk,"
replied the man in the smart, slightly disgusting fedora.
"I'm a home bum now and I need an encampment
and this church has a quaint portico so that's all I can
say I know about it," he mused, picking out teeth.
The rector explained to the newsman that the addled
vagrants used the upstairs church unisex bathroom
to deal hard drugs and stab each other privately with shivs.
"It's so out-of-hand we started locking up the john
after services, but they aren't deterred... I don't know
how to *say this* but, well, one of them started going
number two right on the floor."
She also cataloged further indiscretions:
"They fight each other with toilet brushes
and pick scabs on memorials
then they run off and I think they must
have stolen something. They yank on
the assemblywoman's weave as she's
trying to escape in a cab
and I saw two men in the yard getting naked
(they were pulling off each other's clothes
and biting their own arms to a pulp).
They're sort of angry because we steal
their needles when they go to sleep
so now they're all hunkered down
nested with bottles of pilfered medicine
inserted in their rectums, for safety.
Goldilocks, as she seems
to be known, was once caught
with a dead jay bird, defiled and
tinkling on this ornamental tablet.

I think they have sex with those rusted
objects by the fence corner
and then they spray their tensile blood
on the sunday school kids.
The list goes on!"
The journalist was crying!
It was clear that these interlopers
had crossed a line, invented a far
more perverted line, then crossed
all the way over that one as well.
"And they're meaner and rougher than drunks!"
The assemblywoman yelped from her new post
at the backroom entrance (she was flirting
with a cameraman, pinching bravely at her stockinged legs).
"It's all the last pastor's fault!" she whined
"Radical, he let them in, he wanted them here
and the church is for the needy, sure
but this is beyond the pale, it really is."
When reached for comment on his involvement
with ushering in the cruddy swarms that terrorize
the church, the former associate pastor in question
gave this statement: "As far as my having
personally allowed the indigent in to exhibit
that type of bad behavior: I think that's
a bit disingenuous. I never invited
anyone or any particular constituency
to linger near the portico."

Coping Is Not Poetry

Tell me I'm a mess
and tell me I'm a mess again
tell me money
and inside another attitude
tell me to buy your shit
academic claptrap
and global doggerel
tell me it is worth it
to chew with my mouth
your face
and I will try
to buy
myself out of it.

The Past

Bring me back to what
I wanted not mention what
I need
because every American day
pushes me away from myself
into being a whiny shit
crying out if not for money
then for shelter and for food.

Keep It

There is no debt
in this stricken land
no one, or a darn thing
worked out in rivers of action
to be heard
the sweets for grandma
a kind of sour anarchy
on the lips of the most
delirious. Last
and be a home
without change.

Faith

Faith got me up
to write
this
poem
Faith keeps me
alive
in the
door-
way
Faith is the difference
between greatness
and a
machine gun

even though everything.

Family Values

There is no such thing as hurt
only privilege
and darkness.

There is a warm shoe
you put a penny in
and it opens.

There is no tell
beside our own relenting
and it remembers every day.

Good Grief

It is not as if
God remembers
everything that I say
or that I put to verse.
God gives me grief
and when I speak his name
my tongue falls off.

Marie's Crisis

I shall prescribe you an odd joke
that burrows through the bone
and metastasizes like cancer
burned for good after dreams.

The sighs of the general, rightly
irrelevant; only everything but god
has control
over what death does not encompass.

I dreamt again last night of mother
she was pinning me to the ground
thanking me for not smelling
—Me? thankful she was alive.

Prosody is fascistic, retail morgue
I stole $20 from a drag queen
at Marie's Crisis, then told her
(she was also an oil lawyer).

I told Zachary, "You think this is fun?
You idealize Wojnarowicz? Tell me
how that is fiction if that is what I
am experiencing, right now—*Sob?*"

The vernacular is first a book
then a minister, finally a master
and parched smiles fire long
into the pond of all disasters.

Out of It

The world is Dracula
"I no longer care about art,"
said the askew coquette
pulsing on the trope side of swept
reneging implicit advances
desiring sand and a dirty place.
"If only I could write a nice poem
and make you cry
but offal and humiliation
are the just remains
of my prissy inventory,"
said the process mouse
with a tire in his stomach
combed from anathema
(shocked and monetized).
It is I who thirst! It is I who
remain, listening
not to the drum of my best sight
but to the hundred blizzard
at the mountain base.
Why not?
"Say a prayer,"
said the milquetoast squire:
  Please, O Heavenly Father
    just
   leave me the fuck out of it.

The United States

Because we have found a whole world to stand
behind us, the constituency reigns
that's a sashaying piece of pulchritude
it doesn't matter what we say we are.
The poet's derangement of his senses
but shirks his own responsibilities
to himself, his attention to the world
that, hostile and manic, penetrates us
with the bloody fleece of hegemony.
I shall leave this page unturned forever
a place shall bow to my recompenses
something inside the sex shall detonate
a shuttle floating always lost in fate.
Is there nothing special about my grief?
Each blank line is a directive to me
(I will repeat myself into the grave).
Toward the robes of terminus excels
the southern well of California
discrete and warm, advancing detriment
debased and orchestral solipsism
unbalanced equations in glory's scheme
                    infecting the planet.
What kind of life can I attribute to
Susan, what key unwinds her palimpsest?
As an unruly teen I once coerced
her into doubting her lord's existence
although despite my prodding she never
gave up her claim on his validity.

It doesn't matter so much if the thing
exists as long as it can be of use.
In this, it can be said that poetry
is another coping mechanism.
Disappointment is a photographing
of the state, wreck every time and belong
eternally to love and sacrament
I was once akin to in my country
and in my fellowship with angry ghosts
who broke the glass in terms that diminished.
The grass, the very lawn I walk upon
completes me in my educational
commerce with a disagreeable law.
Be that so far off from begotten points
the air we suck into ourselves, pointless.
We cannot dick around this century
for I am love, there is love in my hair
rise up respectfully and be over.

August Poem

Soon on earth there will be more water
I don't care about or love my father
known pornographers, totes
so out of crest
occurred is irresistibly grim for
an elaborate gay fantasy
resting on the hillock
of a dead media study
the trick for baldness

the devil on your devil's shoulder.

Tall Flower

Call me immediately I
breathe the air promise-
crammed
spring profuse on me
tell me my desire
is dangerously ricked
against my dreams
effectuate my lack
waving stupidity in the arc
lawyering up undignified birds
picturing impress
chewing on the bad faith
of friends
I am writing a book
per pound
in sensual geese, questions
things that matter
this makes no sense to people
except the poor fashion
it's no use
I have lost faith in you
and in the world
you can call me retarded
or a brat, a wall
but you are the true sycophant
who licks tombs
who gurgles on the salient drug

the tall flower of evil offers
if humility looks like this
then take it.

Rimbaud Gave Up

Walk away from this, walk
into Africa into Cancer
breathing life into a century
is silly when you look at it
through a docent glass
the comforting gauze of
giving in to general failure
of letting the spirit and
permitting the social body.
Instruction manuals and
text books cost
much more than poetry
in American dollars
but save the soul
from actual.

Uses

Version me in brightness
I am alone when I am good with myself
nearly everything I do, every conflict
every pettiness or success
makes me imagine
talking with my mother about it
and she's been dead a year on Wednesday
what would she say
she is the only person in my life
that I loved through and through
and however long I outlast her
physically, my knowing her
was probably as good as it gets
and you're just going to have to live with it
my being messy and stupid
in the face of a criminal fast
that makes our own faces
bend the bow toward Bethlehem
soldier, turn out of yourself whenever
the holy water springs out of lake
Chautauqua and carves in Palestine
do not enjoy the mouth around life
writing poetry does not make a dent in it
we have betrayed those who loved us
in ways even they cannot understand
we have colonized the other's other.

A Small Room Full of Light

Is it the red gaul?
My father quietly drives a school bus
we used to be so close to us
in this degenerating heat
nobody thought that this shape would take hold
and anyone took place in that shell
poor bird, your name is
and, for it, be exactly who I am
some poltergeist masturbating in the subway
trying not to be human but to live
there is some flaw in my cause dominion
I continue to exist, ha ha ha
buy me something special, buy me the moon
smash my face into a set of china
do it, nothing, fuck my goddamn brains out.
For there is a bottom reason to this
compunction and dissolution with death
and when I wasn't a child any more
so be it
touch the inventory all wrong
and
          break open.

Opposite Day

You do not come from your mother
you come over an ocean of dearth
and all the lying labor
of the men who walked the earth.
You do not know where you come from
nor the path you take to cause
you do not know the simplest thing
when the world opens its jaws.

Who is she
who was she
who does she hope to be?

I sail on a wave
to a stranger's grave
along the salt and see.

Poem for Nicholas Parks

Dead Nicholas, what
geranium on youth
sad-eyed and sipping
on a twig of skunky pot
could we have waited for
if better and others we
never understood or respected?
We hated public education
and drove off from it
in a ghost car during lunch.
Low, Nick, comes related people
the house has rays and drums
you also made me on
everything else
bird-swallows of a poor rose
cripples and pennies
and dreams retarded and pure.
You wish you had done something more
but you did a lot for me.
I wish I had written a poem for you
when you were alive, well I
as you do, wish so many things.

Entertaining

Pretend nobody will know you
in a hundred years
and you will be right.
I know what money does to love
and what time does to the climate
of where we are or would be.
Nothing, never, never was
never would she.
I'm sorry for your loss
to deconstruct
to learn a fucking word
and then buy into it
and let it be you then now
not so clever, not so much as alive
as where the lived was in it
I put things inside of my house
that I want to keep
and love and the economy
ruins it.
In the end, he said, at least there was that
a torn out property of heart.
Entertain me in the light of my own light.

August Loss

I will look back on it
and say art
made sense the purist
to me when I was
fucked
I've shook the lens
and wart
the roll fur
benign everything
(Whatever your loved
one tells you
do
the opposite).
Loss is not so
complete
that it
does
not
(leave room for suffering).

Blue Moon

Work and sex and
work and sex
time
whatever
the scrim is hard
and pulling
across my deleterious throat.
I am no longer young
all my friends are dead
or dispersed across the continent.
I want art and
then I don't
I want love
but fear death
like having.
Set everything on fire
I have had such experiences
by myself
that if this never works out
at least I will have
my
private joy.

Death in Late Summer

I am brought away
on a wave
of none of your business.
These days, how do you
last these days
how can one man
face society soberly?
Nothing but the belief of the poet
surrounds me in tomorrow
and I've lost it
the cause, the idea
(I die).

How We Do Things

What changes your life
when the summer goes
there's a difference
and poetry is a cripple
with a mouth full of apples
do right by me, write
let me see when the fallow
clock wants as long as it
wants.
Hegemony or some such
burlesque and hoary thing
nudges its boot into the
pregnant flesh of my throat
applies pressure, grunts
"I'm sorry old friend but
that's just not how we do
things around here anymore."

Structure Fire

I have to have faith in my
own feelings and allow
whatever speechless need
that may wrestle through
the boundaries. I have to
be sloppy and crass and broke
to grieve for myself and for
those whom I have loved
that have died. I have to
die a thousand times without
death before death into death
and prelude my honesty with
ungainly doubt lest I fall
on fire into the structure of
compliance.

Music

Genius and life are on their way
in and out at the same time, diseases
and learning and freedom like the
shadow of themselves under
a wet tarp of sexuality and politics.
People saw the words and took hands
who are now not here
and I made a century of loss
out of my failure to deal with it
and be a person
who did feel love
and whose penis stood
hard in the middle of the night.
It does not matter what our name is
you are me.

I Look Back on a Field

Then I was angry

I look back on a field
that I have left behind me

I am so sorry, Christopher
I do not know what
this amounts to.

In us a cancer grows
and makes itself explicit
but

I am no sager nor
am I more capable for it

(I look back on a field).

Fall Rising

First, we met at the Met
I almost jumped out the window
my mom took me for a walk
in her wig
I am just going to read
"What happened to us?"
I am just going to write
everything I can remember
before I became a ward
there is a space shuttle shaped
hole in the ocean
until god gives me
what I want
fills me with an anti-social grace
and pretty boys show me their cock.

It was just a moment in passing
now it's gone.

The Governments

Throw your dresses
into an aching moor
there is something that
prepares us that doesn't
and here I am all
wuthering in your
taste for the governments
send west be a sound
the world it hardly
touches ground
some small palm put
a green into the death
in the brush at the side
yard
dear socialism, my mother
is what I can believe
when I sit down
on this stupid wood bench
legs crossed primly
head stuffed in a newspaper
wracked and half condescendingly
say we all fell from those towers
in image
at the window half glossed over
with the standing of a clasped
cyst who does not have an
opinion, who dares to die
unctuous and in doubt

between the gun and the
whole founding.

If I could destroy something
just to make it real...

Ha

I will be vital?
I will mean something
to the human spirit?
No, I do not like anything
like trees well break them
it far all off it
I was better of before
ha, ha
I have a gun
challenge me
I love, ha
I went shopping
    I love shopping!
Break me, please
please do not ask me
what there is
left to decide
or have been in queer
all of it for sale
even the queer in it
we all woke up
into our own not
like it do you like it
does it become me
to ha

Kate Bush

The lack of justice limits my vocabulary
and prosody springs open unused wells
in my quiet deranged moments, which
are special. The time to express is death
because there is the death that we deny
and then there is the deal we made with
god.

The Moonrise over Wal-Mart

I grew up with a white lung
a joint of marihuana in my teeth
leaning out of the bedroom window
on a winter night
looking past the berm
into ridiculous futures
as if any one would get me through.
My breath hung in the air
so crisp it cut my tongue
my mouth smelled like
a forest of Christmas trees.
Mom had curlers in her hair
dancing around the floral wallpapered
appointments, toes unfurled
into a velvet respite.
Is this what we came here for
in our mud-colored wagon?
(To meet something we
yearn for but need to escape?)
Somehow each inhalation of
pink kitchen corners
and impossible rural routes
accrued into the sum
of what we have to deal with
after years of giving birth
to still and lachrymose figures.
Owning up to myself in
the bog, I think of

my friend from high school
Nicholas
who overdosed in a car
parked in a graveyard
I think of Elinor meeting her god
through a blanket of morphine
I think of Susan
(how each night I left her
drooling in her Hospice bed
and went out in the backyard
to stand in the circle of dirt
where the pool used to be
looking up at the usurious moon
and weeping
as wild bucks sulked around me).
 Let's mile, goddamn it, let's jut.
 Let's find out who was in this boat. "Yeah dad."
 The moonrise over Wal-Mart.

Challenger

When Space Shuttle Challenger broke apart
seventy-three seconds into its flight
(disintegrating over the ocean
leading to the deaths of the crew members
who plummeted into the Atlantic)
the reinforced aluminum cabin
detached in one piece and slowly tumbled
into a ballistic arc then free fall
(and while the forces involved at this stage
were insufficient to cause injury
and the astronauts were very likely
alive and briefly conscious, when they met
the ocean surface the impact was such
that god opened his mouth into the world).

Idumea

Everything is red. The ground is red
the blood   for some
of us there is a future, though I've had
my doubts   for some
of us are haunted by loves beyond love
we walked through the mall or I never
met you   there is a lens
marked terror and when I look through it
all I can can see is my own failure
fleeting as it is, it cannot stand, not against
you, virtuous and muddled motherhood
delighting in a clear day and raked through
by circumstance, left standing, out of force
getting old, having it all taken out of you
surgically, piece by piece, till science
steals away your body, till I can't look
at your picture for the pain, and I can't
remember your voice, till everything gets
burned down to the ashes of an everlasting
love   am I born to die?
yes   but why?
be quiet now but sear a coal-strong fury
through everything within me, every day
there's nothing left and no reason but to
carry the world inside you
        what will become of me?
might I take the voice and the strength
that you left and see the flaming skies?

there is the despair of the heart
and the horror of the spectacle
but they are by no means the same thing.

This is America; or

I love you Susan.

Acknowledgements

I would like to extend boundless gratitude to my first readers, editors, advocates, friends, and spirit animals: CA Conrad, Cecelia Corrigan, Paul Cunningham, Andrew Durbin, Ben Fama, Joshua Furst, the late Rev. Dr. Elinor Hare, Gregory Laynor, Richard Loranger, Brian Marrero, Ryan Doyle May, the late Nicholas Parks, Ben Pease, Robert Snyderman, Bianca Stone, JK Tallon, and Edmund White.

Poems from this series have appeared in the Internet publications *Radioactive Moat*, *EOAGH*, *Poets Touching Trees*, and *Maggy*. The first two books within the series were originally published individually in limited editions. *Poems in June* was published by The Corresponding Society in 2011. *Crush Dream* was published by Radioactive Moat Press in 2012.

Poems in June was written in June 2011. Susan died on August 22nd, 2011. *Crush Dream* was written January to March, 2012. *Challenger* was written April to September, 2012.

Poems in June is dedicated to Robert Synderman. *Crush Dream* is dedicated to Ben Fama. *Challenger* is dedicated to Richard Loranger.

Death & Disaster Series is dedicated to the memory of my mother, Susan.

Illustration by CL Martin

Lonely Christopher is a poet and filmmaker. He is the author of the short story collection *The Mechanics of Homosexual Intercourse*, which was a 2011 selection of Dennis Cooper's Little House on the Bowery imprint of Akashic Books. His plays have been produced in New York City and China. He wrote and directed the feature film *MOM* (Cavazos Films, 2013) and his stories have been adapted for the screen in Canada and France. He lives in Brooklyn.